John Mason Neale

Hymns suitable for invalids

Being a selection of hymns appropriate to the sickroom

John Mason Neale

Hymns suitable for invalids
Being a selection of hymns appropriate to the sickroom

ISBN/EAN: 9783741198540

Manufactured in Europe, USA, Canada, Australia, Japa

Cover: Foto ©Angelika Wolter / pixelio.de

Manufactured and distributed by brebook publishing software
(www.brebook.com)

John Mason Neale

Hymns suitable for invalids

Hymns suitable for Invalids:

BEING A SELECTION OF

Hymns appropriate to the Sick-Room,

ORIGINAL OR TRANSLATED,

BY

THE LATE REV. J. M. NEALE, D.D.,

WARDEN OF SACKVILLE COLLEGE,

WITH

PREFACE BY R. F. LITTLEDALE, LL.D.

London:

J. T. HAYES, LYALL PLACE, EATON SQUARE.

PREFACE.

THE Hymns in this small collection are drawn from
different volumes of Sacred Poetry by the late Dr. NEALE,
The Hymn "LORD JESUS, Who for us didst bear."
is reprinted here from the *Priest's Prayer Book*, for
which it was originally written, and which owes so much
to Dr. Neale's criticisms and suggestions.

That the *Readings for the Aged* and several of the
Hymns which he has left us have proved singularly ac-
ceptable and soothing at sick and dying beds, whatever
the rank or age of the sufferer might be, is known to the
experience of very many of those whose duties call them
amidst such scenes. And that it shoud be so forms by
no means the least item in the claims which his memory

has upon our gratitude and affection. It is granted to but few to alleviate in any appreaciable degree the mental and spiritual pain which so often accompany physical disease, and we cannot rate too highly those who rank amongst them. If the poems here gathered together help forward that work of consolation, no more happy result could have been desired from them by their lamented writer. And if they shall be crowned who have visited a few of the sick with words of hope and comfort, what shall be his reward who has thus ministered to thousands of aching hearts!

R. F. L.

London, Michaelmas Day, 1866.

CONTENTS.

CONTENTS.

The Invalid's Hymn-Book.

ART THOU WEARY?

ART thou weary, art thou languid,
    Art thou sore distrest?
" Come to me"—saith One—" and coming,
    Be at rest !"

Hath He marks to lead me to Him,
    If He be my Guide?
" In His Feet and Hands are Wound-prints,
    And His Side."

Is there Diadem, as Monarch,
    That His brow adorns?
" Yea, a Crown, in very surety,
    But of Thorns !"

If I find Him, if I follow,
    What His guerdon here?
" Many a sorrow, many a labour,
        Many a tear."

If I still hold closely to Him,
    What hath He at last?
" Sorrow vanquish'd, labour ended,
        Jordan past!"

If I ask Him to receive me,
    Will He say me nay?
" Not till earth, and not till heaven
        Pass away!"

Finding, following, keeping, struggling,
    Is He sure to bless?
" Angels, Martyrs, Prophets, Virgins,
        Answer, Yes!"

AND WILT THOU PARDON, LORD?

AND wilt Thou pardon, LORD,
    A sinner such as I?
Although Thy book his crimes record
    Of such a crimson dye?

So deep are they engrav'd,—
    So terrible their fear,
The righteous scarcely shall be sav'd,
    And where shall I appear?

My soul, make all things known
    To Him Who all things sees:
That so the LAMB may yet atone
    For thine iniquities.

O Thou, Physician blest,
Make clean my guilty soul!
And me, by many a sin oppress'd,
Restore and keep me whole!

I know not how to praise
Thy mercy and Thy love:
But deign Thy servant to upraise,
And I shall learn above!

THAT FEARFUL DAY.

———

THAT fearful Day, that-Day of speechless
  dread;
When Thou shalt come to judge the quick
  and dead——
    I shudder to foresee,
    O GOD! what then shall be!

When Thou shalt come, angelic legions round,
With thousand thousands, and with trumpet
  sound;
    CHRIST, grant me in the air
    With saints to meet Thee there!

Weep, O my soul, ere that great hour and day,
When GOD shall shine in manifest array,

Thy sin, that thou may'st be
In that strict judgment free!

The terror!—hell-fire fierce and unsufficed:
The bitter worm: the gnashing teeth:—O
  Christ,
     Forgive, remit, protect;
     And set me with the elect!

That I may hear the blessed voice that calls
The righteous to the joys of heavenly halls:
     And, King of Heaven, may reach
     The realm that passeth speech!

Enter Thou not in judgment with each deed,
Nor each intent and thought in strictness
  read:
     Forgive, and save me then,
     O Thou That lovest men!

Thee, One in Three blest Persons! LORD o'er
all!
Essence of essence, Power of power, we call!
Save us, O FATHER, SON,
And SPIRIT, ever one!

JESU, NAME ALL NAMES ABOVE.

Jesu, Name all names above,
    Jesu, best and dearest,
Jesu, Fount of perfect love,
    Holiest, tenderest, nearest;
Jesu, Source of grace completest,
Jesu purest, Jesu sweetest,
    Jesu, Well of power Divine,
    Make me, keep me, seal me Thine!

Jesu, open me the gate
    That of old he enter'd,
Who, in that most lost estate,
    Wholly on Thee ventur'd;

Thou, Whose Wounds are ever pleading,
And Thy Passion interceding,
    From my misery let me rise
    To a Home in Paradise !

Thou didst call the Prodigal :
    Thou didst pardon Mary :
Thou, Whose words can never fall,
    Love can never vary :
Lord, to heal my lost condition
Give—for Thou can'st give—contrition ;
    Thou canst pardon all mine ill
    If Thou wilt : O say, " I will !"

Woe, that I have turned aside
    After fleshly pleasure !
Woe, that I have never tried
    For the Heavenly Treasure !

Treasure, safe in Home supernal ;
Incorruptible, eternal !
  Treasure no less price hath won
  Than the Passion of The SON !

JESU, crown'd with Thorns for me,
  Scourged for my transgression,
Witnessing, through agony,
  That Thy good confession !
JESU, clad in purple raiment,
For my evils making payment ;
  Let not all Thy woe and pain,
  Let not Calvary, be in vain !

When I reach Death's bitter sea,
  And its waves roll higher,
· Help the more forsaking me
  As the storm draws nigher :

Jesu, leave me not to languish,
Helpless, hopeless, full of anguish!
  Tell me,—" Verily I say,
  Thou shalt be with Me to-day!"

GOD COMES.

God comes;—and who shall stand before His
    fear ?
Who bide His Presence, when He draweth
    near ?
        My soul, my soul, prepare
        To kneel before Him there !

Haste,—weep,—be reconciled to Him before
The fearful judgment knocketh at the door :
        Where, in the Judge's eyes,
        All bare and naked lies.

Have mercy, Lord; have mercy, Lord, I cry,
When with Thine angels Thou appear'st on
    high :

And each shall doom inherit,
According to his merit.

How can I bear Thy fearful anger, LORD?
I, that so often have transgressed Thy word?
    But put my sins away,
    And spare me in that day!

O miserable soul, return, lament,
Ere earthly converse end, and life be spent:
    Ere, time for sorrow o'er,
    The Bridegroom close the door!

Yea, I have sinned, as no man sinned beside:
With more than human guilt my soul is
    dyed:
    But spare, and save me here,
    Before that day appear!

Three Persons in One Essence uncreate,
On Whom, both Three and One, our praises
  wait,
          Give everlasting light
          To them that sing Thy might!

JERUSALEM, MY HAPPY HOME.

———

JERUSALEM! my happy Home!
  When shall I come to thee?
When shall my sorrows have an end?
  Thy joys when shall I see?

O happy harbour of the saints,
  O sweet and pleasant soil,
In thee no sorrow may be found,
  No grief, no care, no toil!

In thee no sickness may be seen,
  No hurt, no ache, no sore;
There is no death, nor ugly dole,
  But Life for evermore.

No dampish mist is seen in thee,
    No cold nor darksome night ;
There every soul shines as the sun ;
    There GOD Himself gives light.

There lust and lucre cannot dwell,
    There envy bears no sway ;
There is no hunger, heat, nor cold
    But pleasure every way.

Jerusalem ! Jerusalem !
    GOD grant I once may see
Thy endless joys, and of the same
    Partaker aye to be !

II.

JERUSALEM ! my happy Home !
    When shall I come to thee ?

When shall my sorrows have an end ?
  Thy joys when shall I see ?

Thy walls are made of precious stones,
  Thy bulwarks diamonds square,
Thy gates are of right orient pearl,
  Exceeding rich and rare.

Thy turrets and thy pinnacles
  With carbuncles do shine ;
Thy very streets are paved with gold,
  Surpassing clear and fine.

Thy houses are of ivory,
  Thy windows crystal clear ;
Thy tiles are made of beaten gold ;
  —O GOD, that I were there !

Within thy gates doth nothing come
  That is not passing clean ;

No spider's web, no dirt, no dust,
    No filth may there be seen.

Ah, my sweet Home, Jerusalem,
    ˙Would GOD I were in thee!
Would GOD my woes were at an end,
    Thy joys that I might see!

III.

JERUSALEM! my happy Home!
    When shall I come to thee?
When shall my sorrows have an end?
    Thy joys when shall I see?

Thy saints are crowned with glory great,
    They see GOD face to face;
They triumph still, they still rejoice;
    Most happy is their case.

We that are here in banishment
    Continually do moan;
We sigh and sob, we weep and wail,
    Perpetually we groan.

Our sweet is mixed with bitter gall,
    Our pleasure is but pain;
Our joys scarce last the looking on,
    Our sorrows still remain.

But there they live in such delight,
    Such pleasure and such play,
As that to them a thousand years
    Doth seem as yesterday.

Jerusalem! Jerusalem!
    GOD grant I once may see
Thy endless joys, and of the same
    Partaker aye to be!

IV.

JERUSALEM! my happy Home!
    When shall I come to thee?
When shall my sorrows have an end?
    Thy joys when shall I see?

Thy vineyards and thy orchards are
    Most beautiful and fair,
Full furnished with trees and fruits,
    Exceeding rich and rare.

Thy gardens and thy gallant walks
    Continually are green;
There grow such sweet and pleasant flowers
    As nowhere else are seen.

There nectar and ambrosia flow;
    There, musk and civet sweet;

There many a fair and dainty drug
  Are trodden under feet.

There cinnamon, there sugar grow,
  There nard and balm abound;
What tongue can tell or heart contain
  The joys that there are found?

Quite through the streets, with silver sound,
  The Flood of Life doth flow;
Upon whose banks, on every side,
  The Wood of Life doth grow.

Ah, my sweet Home Jerusalem,
  Would GOD I were in thee!
Would GOD my woes were at an end,
  Thy joys that I might see!

V.

Jerusalem! my happy Home!
   When shall I come to thee?
When shall my sorrows have an end?
   Thy joys when shall I see?

There trees for evermore bear fruit,
   And evermore do spring;
There evermore the angels sit,
   And evermore do sing.

There David stands, with harp in hands,
   As master of the quire;
Ten thousand times that man were blest,
   That might this music hear!

Our Lady sings *Magnificat*,
   With tones surpassing sweet;

And all the Virgins bear their part,
Sitting about her feet.

Te Deum doth Saint Ambrose sing,
Saint Austin doth the like ;
Old Simeon and Zachary
Have not their songs to seek.

There Magdalene hath left her moan,
And cheerfully doth sing
With blessed Saints, whose harmony
In every street doth ring.

Jerusalem ! my happy Home !
Would GOD I were in thee !
Would GOD my woes were at an end,
Thy joys that I might see !

FIERCE WAS THE WILD BILLOW.

FIERCE was the wild billow ;
    Dark was the night ;
Oars labour'd heavily ;
    Foam glimmer'd white ;
Trembled the mariners ;
    Peril was high ;
Then said the GOD of GOD,
    —" Peace ! It is I ! "

Ridge of the mountain-wave,
    Lower thy crest !
Wail of Euroclydon,
    Be thou at rest !

Sorrow can never be,—
  Darkness must fly,—
Where saith the Light of Light,
  —" Peace! It is I!"

Jesu, Deliverer!
  Come Thou to me:
Soothe Thou my voyaging
  Over Life's sea!
Thou, when the storm of Death
  Roars, sweeping by,
Whisper, O Truth of Truth!
  —" Peace! It is I!"

THE DAY IS NEAR.

The Day is near, the Judgment is at hand,
Awake, my soul, awake, and ready stand!
Where chiefs shall go with them that filled
   the throne,
Where rich and poor the same tribunal own ;
     And every thought and deed
     Shall find its righteous meed.

There with the sheep the shepherd of the fold
Shall stand together ; there the young and old ;
Master and slave one doom shall undergo ;
Widow and maiden one tribunal know.
     O woe, oh woe to them
     Whom lawless lives condemn !

That Judgment-seat, impartial in decree,
Accepts no bribe, admits no subtilty:
No orator persuasion may exert,
No perjured witness wrong to right convert:
But all things, hid in night,
Shall then be dragged to light.

Let me not enter in the land of woe;
Let me not realms of outer darkness know!
Nor from the wedding-feast reject Thou
me,
For my soiled vest of immortality;
Bound hand and foot, and cast
In anguish that shall last!

When Thou, the nations ranged on either
side,
The righteous from the sinners shalt divide,

Then give me to be found amongst Thy
    sheep,
Then from the goats Thy trembling servant
    keep:
      That I may hear the voice
      That bids Thy Saints rejoice!

When righteous inquisition shall be made,
And the books opened, and the thrones ar-
    rayed,
My soul, what plea to shield Thee canst
    thou know,
Who hast no fruit of righteousness to show,
      No holy deeds to bring
      To CHRIST the LORD and King?

I hear the rich man's wail and bitter cry,
Out of the torments of eternity;

I know, beholding that devouring flame,
My guilt and condemnation are the same ;
    And spare me, LORD, I say,
    In that great Judgment Day !

The WORD and SPIRIT, with the FATHER
  One,
One Light and emanation of One Sun,
The WORD by generation, we adore,
The SPIRIT by procession, evermore ;
    And with creation raise
    The thankful hymn of praise.

ARE THY TOILS.

———

ARE thy toils and woes increasing ?
Are the Foe's attacks unceasing ?
  Look with Faith unclouded,
  Gaze with eyes unshrouded,
   On the Cross !

Dost thou fear that strictest trial ?
Tremblest thou at CHRIST's denial ?
  Never rest without it,
  Clasp thine hands about it,
  —That dear Cross !

Diabolic legions press thee ?
Thoughts and works of sin distress thee ?

It shall chase all terror,
It shall right all error,
   That sweet Cross !

Draw'st thou nigh to Jordan's river ?
Should'st thou tremble ? Need'st thou quiver ?
   No ! if by it lying,—
   No ! if on it dying,—
    On the Cross !

Say then,—" Master, while I cherish
That sweet hope, I cannot perish !
   After this life's story,
   Give Thou me the glory
    For the Cross ! "

THE LORD DRAWS NIGH.

THE LORD draws nigh, the righteous Throne's
  Assesssor,
The just to save, to punish the transgressor :
      Weep we, and mourn, and pray,
      Regardful of that day ;
When all the secrets of all hearts shall be
Lit with the blaze of full eternity.

Clouds and thick darkness o'er the Mount
  assembling,
Moses beheld the Eternal's glory, trembling :
      And yet he might but see
      GOD's feebler Majesty.

And I—I needs must view His fullest Face:
O spare me, LORD! O take me to Thy
grace!

David of old beheld, in speechless terror,
The session of the Judge—the doom of error:
     And what have I to plead
     For mercy in my need?
Nothing save this: O grant me yet to be,
Ere that day come, renewed and true to
Thee!

Here, fires of deep damnation roar and glitter:
The worm is deathless, and the cup is bitter.
     There, day that hath no morrow,
     And joy that hath no sorrow:
And who so blest that he shall fly the abyss,
Rais'd up to GOD's Right Hand, and speech-
less bliss!

My soul with many an act of sin is wounded :
With mortal weakness is my frame sur-
rounded !
My life is well-nigh o'er :
The Judge is at the door :
How wilt thou, miserable spirit, fare,
What time He sends His summons through
the air ?

From the Rhythm of Bernard de Morlaix.

I.

THE WORLD IS VERY EVIL.

THE world is very evil;
　　The times are waxing late:
Be sober and keep vigil;
　　The Judge is at the gate:
The Judge That comes in mercy,
　　The Judge That comes with might,
To terminate the evil,
　　To diadem the right.
When the just and gentle Monarch
　　Shall summon from the tomb,
Let Man, the guilty, tremble,
　　For Man, the GOD, shall doom.

Arise, arise, good Christian,
  Let right to wrong succeed ;
Let penitential sorrow
  To heavenly gladness lead ;
To the light that hath no evening,
  That knows nor moon nor sun,
The light so new and golden,
  The light that is but one.
And when the Sole-Begotten
  Shall render up once more
The kingdom to the FATHER
  Whose own it was before,—
Then glory yet unheard of
  Shall shed abroad its ray,
Resolving all enigmas,
  An endless Sabbath-day.
Strive, man, to win that glory ;
  Toil, man, to gain that light ;

Send hope before to grasp it,
  Till hope be lost in sight :
Till JESUS gives the portion
  Those blessed souls to fill,
The insatiate, yet satisfied,
  The full, yet craving still.
That fulness and that craving
  Alike are free from pain,
Where thou, midst heavenly citizens,
  A home like theirs shall gain.

II.

BRIEF LIFE IS HERE OUR PORTION.

Brief life is here our portion;
  Brief sorrow, short-lived care;
The life that knows no ending,
  The tearless life, is *There*.

O happy retribution !
  Short toil, eternal rest ;
For mortals and for sinners
  A mansion with the blest !
That we should look, poor wand'rers,
  To have our home on high !
That worms should seek for dwellings
  Beyond the starry sky !
To all one happy guerdon
  Of one celestial grace ;
For all, for all, who mourn their fall,
  Is one eternal place :
And martyrdom hath roses
  Upon that heavenly ground :
And white and virgin lilies
  For virgin-souls abound.
Their grief is turned to pleasure ;
  Such pleasure, as below

No human voice can utter,
  No human heart can know :
And after fleshly scandal,
  And after this world's night,
And after storm and whirlwind,
  In calm, and joy, and light.
And now we fight the battle,
  But then shall wear the crown
Of full and everlasting
  And passionless renown ;
And now we watch and struggle,
  And now we live in hope,
And Syon, in her anguish,
  With Babylon must cope :
But He Whom now we trust in
  Shall then be seen and known,
And they that know and see Him
  Shall have Him for their own.

The miserable pleasures
　　Of the body shall decay :
The bland and flattering struggles
　　Of the flesh shall pass away :
And none shall there be jealous ;
　　And none shall there contend ;
Fraud, clamour, guile—what say I ?
　　—All ill, all ill shall end !
And there is David's Fountain,
　　And life in fullest glow,
And there the light is golden,
　　And milk and honey flow :
The light that hath no evening,
　　The health that hath no sore,
The life that hath no ending,
　　But lasteth evermore.

III.

FOR THEE, O DEAR DEAR COUNTRY.

For thee, O dear dear Country!
   Mine eyes their vigils keep;
For very love, beholding
   Thy happy name, they weep:
The mention of thy glory
   Is unction to the breast,
And medicine in sickness,
   And love, and life and rest.
O one, O onely Mansion!
   O Paradise of Joy!
Where tears are ever-banished,
   And smiles have no alloy:
Beside thy living waters
   All plants are, great and small,
The cedar of the forest,
   The hyssop of the wall:

With jaspers glow thy bulwarks;
  Thy streets with emeralds blaze;
The sardius and the topaz
  Unite in thee their rays;
Thine ageless walls are bonded
  With amethyst unpriced :
Thy Saints build up its fabric,
  And the corner-stone is CHRIST.
The Cross is all thy splendour,
  The Crucified thy praise:
His laud and benediction
  Thy ransomed people raise:
JESUS, the Gem of Beauty,
  True GOD and Man, they sing:
The never-failing Garden,
  The ever-golden Ring;
The Door, the Pledge, the Husband,
  The Guardian of His Court :.

The Day-star of salvation,
　The Porter and the Port.
Thou hast no shore, fair ocean !
　Thou hast no time, bright day !
Dear fountain of refreshment
　To pilgrims far away !
Upon the Rock of Ages
　They raise thy holy tower :
Thine is the victor's laurel,
　And thine the golden dower :
Thou feel'st in mystic rapture,
　O Bride that know'st no guile,
The Prince's sweetest kisses,
　The Prince's loveliest smile :
Unfading lilies, bracelets
　Of living pearl, thine own ;
The LAMB is ever near thee,
　The Bridegroom thine alone :

The Crown is He to guerdon
  The Buckler to protect,
And He Himself the Mansion,
  And He the Architect.
The only art thou needest,
  Thanksgiving for thy lot :
The only joy thou seekest,
  The Life where Death is not :
And all thine endless leisure
  In sweetest accents sings,
The ill that was thy merit,—
  The wealth that is thy King's !

IV.

JERUSALEM THE GOLDEN.

JERUSALEM THE GOLDEN,
  WITH MILK AND HONEY BLEST,

BENEATH THY CONTEMPLATION
  SINK HEART AND VOICE OPPRESSED:
I KNOW NOT, O I KNOW NOT,
  WHAT SOCIAL JOYS ARE THERE;
WHAT RADIANCY OF GLORY,
  WHAT LIGHT BEYOND COMPARE!
AND WHEN I FAIN WOULD SING THEM,
  MY SPIRIT FAILS AND FAINTS,—
AND VAINLY WOULD IT IMAGE
  THE ASSEMBLY OF THE SAINTS.
THEY STAND, THOSE HALLS OF SYON,
  CONJUBILANT WITH SONG,
AND BRIGHT WITH MANY AN ANGEL,
  AND ALL THE MARTYR THRONG:
THE PRINCE IS EVER IN THEM;
  THE DAYLIGHT IS SERENE;
THE PASTURES OF THE BLESSED
  ARE DECKED IN GLORIOUS SHEEN.

THERE IS THE THRONE OF DAVID,—
    AND THERE, FROM CARE RELEASED,
THE SONG OF THEM THAT TRIUMPH,
    THE SHOUT OF THEM THAT FEAST;
AND THEY WHO, WITH THEIR LEADER,
    HAVE CONQUERED IN THE FIGHT,
FOR EVER AND FOR EVER
    ARE CLAD IN ROBES OF WHITE.

V.

JERUSALEM THE GLORIOUS.

Jerusalem the glorious!
    The glory of the Elect!
O dear and future vision
    That eager hearts expect:
Even now by faith I see thee:
    Even here thy walls discern:

To thee my thoughts are kindled,
And strive and pant and yearn :
Jerusalem the onely,
That look'st from heaven below,
In thee is all my glory ;
In me is all my woe ;
And though my body may not,
My spirit seeks thee fain,
. Till flesh and earth return me
To earth and flesh again.
O none can tell thy bulwarks,
How gloriously they rise :
O none can tell thy capitals
Of beautiful device :
Thy loveliness oppresses
All human thought and heart :
And none, O peace, O Syon,
Can sing thee as thou art.

O fields that know no sorrow;
  O state that fears no strife!
O princely bow'rs! O land of flow'rs!
  O Realm and Home of life!

                                    •

Jerusalem, exulting
  On that securest shore,
I hope thee, wish thee, sing thee,
  And love thee evermore!
I ask not for my merit :
  I seek not to deny
My merit is destruction,
  A child of wrath am I :
But yet with Faith I venture
  And Hope upon my way;
For those perennial guerdons
  I labour night and day.

The Best and Dearest FATHER
  Who made me and Who saved,
Bore with me in defilement,
  And from defilement laved:
When in His strength I struggle,
  For every joy I leap;
When in my sin I totter,
  I weep, or try to weep:
And grace, sweet grace celestial,
  Shall all its love display,
And David's Royal Fountain,
  Purge every sin away.

O mine, my Golden Syon!
  O lovelier far than gold!
With laurel-girt battalions,
  And safe victorious fold:

E

O sweet and blessed Country,
    Shall I ever see thy face?
O sweet and blessed Country,
    Shall I ever win thy grace?
I *have* the hope within me
    To comfort and to bless!
Shall I ever win the prize itself?
    O tell me, tell me, Yes!

Exult, O dust and ashes!
    The LORD shall be thy part:
His only, His for ever,
    Thou shalt be, and thou art!
Exult, O dust and ashes!
    The LORD shall be thy part:
His only, His for ever,
    Thou shalt be, and thou art!

COUNT NOT.

———

" Count not," the Lord's Apostle saith,
   Who knew afflictions' sting,
" The fiery trial of your faith
   As an unwonted thing."
Yea, rather, Christ Himself would teach
   His people, ere He went,
That they were mark'd for grief by each
   Thrice-blessed Sacrament.

When we, endued with power on high,
   Began to live afresh,
We vowed our wills to mortify,
   And crucify the flesh ;

To count all earthly gain as loss,
 All earthly honour shame;
And we were strengthened with the Cross,
 That we might bear the same.

Doth not the Altar call our thought
 To His expiring breath?
The woes that our salvation bought,
 The love as strong as death.
His precious Body makes not whole
 Till broken on the Wood:
The Chalice could not cleanse our soul,
 Except it were His Blood.

A Master suffering on the Tree,
 A servant at his ease!
Far, O Thou LORD of Calvary,
 Such thoughts and hopes as these!

ın us, and by us, every day,
  Thy holy will be done,
Till Thou shalt call our soul away,
  " Eternal Three in One."   Amen.

'TIS BUT A FILM.

'TIS but a film of flesh divides
Us from the heav'nly place ;
'Tis heaven to be where GOD resides,
And see Him face to face.

Our GOD is everywhere around ;
But, while we sojourn here,
Thick mists from earth the sense confound
And heaven may not appear.

But could we lay the body by,
And wash our eye-sight clean,—
Then look into the boundless sky,
How different 'twould be seen !

What now is void and silent space
Were full and vocal then ;
Its habitants a heavenly race
Though once our brother men.

Our brethren once, our brethren now,
Still knit in holy love ;
We praise and serve Him here below,
They praise and serve above.

OH! HAPPY LAND ABOVE.

OH ! happy Land above !
Thy soul would fain be there ;
A Land of life and love,
Unsullied with a tear.

O happy men, whose toil
Hath gain'd those hills of light,
Put off this mortal coil,
For natures heavenly bright !

Their work on earth is wrought,
Their race of trial run,
The field of glory fought
—And oh ! the battle won.

My soul would fain be there !
To Him I've lov'd below,
To shining worlds,—how fair
No human heart may know,—

From sighs and sorrowing,
From frail and feeble clay,
Oh, had I a dove's wing,
How quickly I'd away !

EYE HATH NEVER.

———

Eye hath never seen the glory;
  Ear hath never heard the song;
Heart of man can never image
  What good things to them belong,
Who have loved the Lord of beauty,
  While they dwelt in this world's throng.

If the body, once made glorious,
  Such high gifts and bright shall own,
What the beatification
  Of the spirits round the Throne,
When in perfect revelation
  Shall the Bridegroom's Face be shown?

There the soul in fullest tenour,
    Graspeth wisdom's total round ;
There in loveliest peace and concord
    With each sister soul is bound ;
And, for shame receiving double,
    . Sits, with perfect honour crowned.

O how full, how heaped the rapture—
    O how blest, how high the soul,—
When on every side around her
    Torrents of such pleasure roll !
Nothing this way, nothing that way,
    Lacking to the perfect whole.

Every sense in every fibre
    There, beholding GOD, shall thrill ;
All the intellectual vigour
    Clearly comprehend Him still ;

Whom embracing unitively,
  Thou shalt love with perfect will.

Yield not then to fear or weeping,
  O thou soul of little faith !
If it chance that many travails
  Should assail, as Scripture saith ;
Or if manifold temptations
  Of the fiend should work thee scathe. .

Lo ! thou hearest that the sufferings
  Of the present world are not
Worth compare the weight of glory
  That shall be thy future lot ;
Weight eternal, weight exceeding ;
  Endless joy and pain forgot.   Amen.

LORD JESU, WHO FOR US DIDST BEAR.

Lord Jesu, Who for us didst bear
    Such anguish and distress,
And all our many trials share,
    And all our sicknesses.

For this dear end Thou bearest woe,
    That by such pain and shame
Thy people's sufferings Thou might'st know,
    As having felt the same.

Thou well canst make our easier bed,
    To such a hard one bound;
Thou pitiest every aching head,
    For Thine with thorns was crowned.

Thou feltest anguish long and keen,
  And weakness at its worst;
Thou know'st what burning fevers mean,
  For Thou hast said, " I thirst."

Thine hands made whole the child from harm,
  Whom demons sore oppress'd;
And children taken in Thine Arms,
  By Thy dear words were blest.

No pulse that moved, no breath that stirred,
  Her life had reached its close;
Talitha cumi was Thy word,
  And straight the maid arose.

Thou chosest innocents to be
  First martyrs here below;
They gave their little lives for Thee,
  Whose Name they could not know.

Thousands since then have learned to bear
  The worst that pain could do ;
In Thine affliction having share,
  But in Thy glory too.

Thou knowest all my future lot,
  Sweet Mary's sweetest SON ;
O raise me up again—yet not
  My will, but Thine be done.

O raise me up to be Thine own,
  Or, if Thou take me hence,
Give me a place beneath Thy throne,
  Among the Innocents.

J. SWIFT, 55, King Street, Regent Street, W.

WORKS BY REV. DR. NEALE.

The LAST TWO WORKS, on his SICK BED, of the late Rev. J. M. NEALE, D.D., Sackville College.

Price 2s. 6d.; by post 2s. 9d.,

ORIGINAL SEQUENCES, HYMNS, and other ECCLESIASTICAL VERSES.

Also, price 1s.; by post 1s. 2d.

STABAT MATER SPECIOSA : Full of Beauty stood the Mother. (Never hitherto Translated.)

Third Edition, price 2s. 6d., by post 2s. 7d.

The HYMNS of the EASTERN CHURCH.

"The *only* English versions of any part of the treasures of Oriental Hymnology."—*Preface.*

Price 1s. 6d.; by post 1s. 7d.

HYMNS on the JOYS and GLORIES of PARADISE.

Price 4s.; by post 4s. 2d.

The TRANSLATIONS of the PRIMITIVE LITURGIES of S. MARK, S. JAMES, S. CLEMENT, S. CHRYSOSTOM, and S. BASIL.

Price 6s.; by post 6s. 2d.

NOTES, Ecclesiological and Picturesque, on DALMATIA, CROATIA, ISTRIA, STYRIA, and MONTENEGRO.

Price 6d.; by post 7d. (the Profits for the "NEALE MEMORIAL" FUND).

A SERMON on the DEATH of the Rev. J. M. NEALE. By Rev. E. MALLESON, Baldersby.

J. T. HAYES, LYALL PLACE.

www.ingramcontent.com/pod-product-compliance
Lightning Source LLC
Chambersburg PA
CBHW020245090426
42735CB00010B/1847